C U T A W A Y

JET
LINERS

JON RICHARDS

5526

COPPER BEECH BOOKS
BROOKFIELD, CONNECTICUT

© Aladdin Books Ltd 1998

*Designed and
produced by*
Aladdin Books Ltd
28 Percy Street
London W1P 0LD

*First published in
the United States in 1998 by*
Copper Beech Books,
an imprint of
The Millbrook Press
2 Old New Milford Road
Brookfield, Connecticut 06804

Editor
Simon Beecroft
Consultant
Colin Uttley
Design
David West
Children's Book Design
Designer
Robert Perry
Illustrators
Simon Tegg & Mike Saunders
Picture Research
Brooks Krikler Research

**Library of Congress
Cataloging-in-Publication Data**
Richards, Jon, 1970-
Jetliners / by Jon Richards ; illustrated
by Simon Tegg.
p. cm. — (Cutaway)
Includes index.
Summary: Examines the cockpit,
passenger cabin, engine, and
other aspects of some of the
world's largest jetliners and explains
how they have changed over
the years from small aircraft to
today's jumbo jets.
ISBN 0-7613-7044-3 (tr. hardcover).
— ISBN 0-7613-0850-4 (lib. bdg.)
1. Jet transporters—Juvenile literature.
[1. Jet transporters.] I. Tegg,
Simon, ill. II. Title. III. Series.
TL685.7.653 1998   98-16919
629.33'349—dc21   CIP AC

CONTENTS

INTRODUCTION

The world's first jetliner entered service a little under fifty years ago. In the short space of time since then, jetliners have improved, and now carry people to all corners of the globe.

They also come in all shapes and sizes. These range from tiny business jets that can only carry a few people over a short distance, to huge jumbo jets that can carry hundreds of people to the other side of the world.

Going up and down

These parts of the wing are called ailerons. The pilot could move the ailerons up and down to make the plane bank or turn.

Flight deck

The flight crew sat in the flight deck at the front of the plane. The flight crew of a 707 was made up of the pilot, first officer, and the flight engineer.

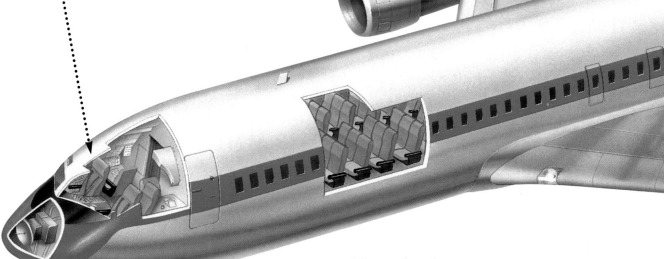

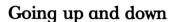

Nosewheels

The nosewheels sat under the front of the plane. When the plane was in the air they were tucked up inside the plane's body.

BOEING 707

The first experimental jet-powered plane flew in 1939. However, it was another 15 years before planes powered by jets

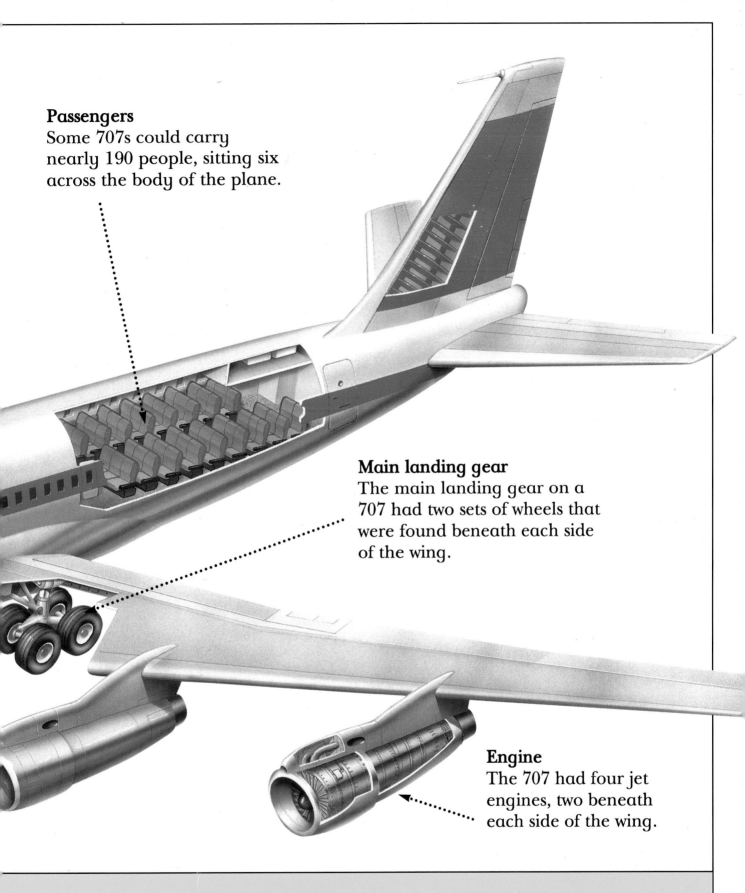

Passengers
Some 707s could carry
nearly 190 people, sitting six
across the body of the plane.

Main landing gear
The main landing gear on a
707 had two sets of wheels that
were found beneath each side
of the wing.

Engine
The 707 had four jet
engines, two beneath
each side of the wing.

carried passengers all over the
world. One of the earliest jet
airliners to go into service was
the Boeing 707. It was first used
in 1958 by Pan American
Airways to carry people across
the Atlantic Ocean between
Europe and the United States.

It takes a lot to

Designing

Aircraft designers need to create a plane that meets the needs of an airline and its passengers. The designers can use a computer to help draw what the plane will look like (*left*).

Giant jigsaw

The parts of a jet airliner are built separately and then put together like the pieces of an enormous jigsaw puzzle (*below*).

build a jetliner.

Testing the engine

Jet engines must work for many hours, carrying a plane over very long distances. A lot of checks and tests are carried out to make sure that the jet engines work without developing problems (*right*).

Test flying

Once the plane has been built it must be tested to see how it flies. Pilots will push the plane to its limits to see how well it flies in extreme conditions in the air (*above*).

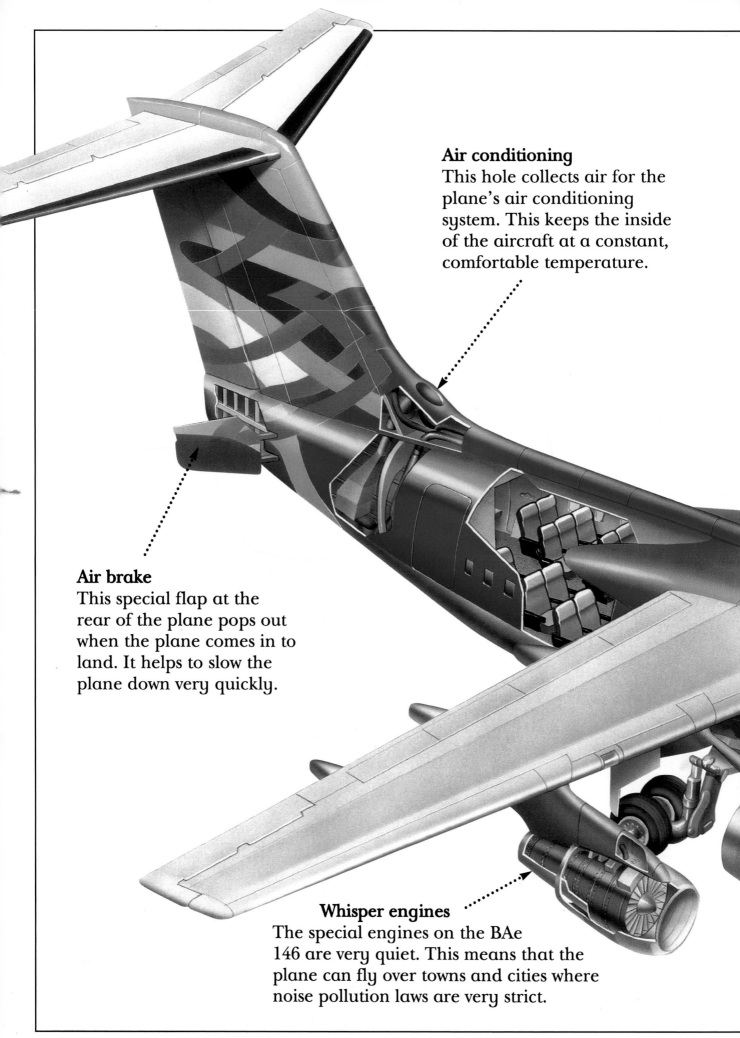

Air conditioning
This hole collects air for the plane's air conditioning system. This keeps the inside of the aircraft at a constant, comfortable temperature.

Air brake
This special flap at the rear of the plane pops out when the plane comes in to land. It helps to slow the plane down very quickly.

Whisper engines
The special engines on the BAe 146 are very quiet. This means that the plane can fly over towns and cities where noise pollution laws are very strict.

High wing
The wing on this plane is set on top of the body. Compare it with the other planes in the book.

SHORT-HAUL JET

Not all jet airliners need to be very big, or fly very long distances. This jet can only carry about 100 people. It is known as a short-haul jet because it is only used to carry passengers on short flights. It is called the British Aerospace (BAe) 146. Its special design allows it to take off and land using very short runways — a jumbo jet needs a runway more than twice as long as the one used by this jet! This makes it an ideal plane for inner-city airports.

Radar
The radar at the front of the aircraft tells the pilots where they are going, which other planes are in the area, or what the weather is like up ahead.

A jetliner has many

In control

The flight crew sit on the flight deck at the front of the plane (*above*). In front of them are the controls and dials that help them to fly the plane.

The galley

This is where the food and drinks are stored. These are delivered to the passengers using special carts (*left*).

different parts to it.

Sitting comfortably

The passengers sit in rows of seats in the passenger cabin. These seats can have televisions to entertain the passengers (*left*) or they can lean back to let the passengers sleep.

The cargo hold

The large space beneath the passenger cabin is used to store the passengers' luggage during the flight. It can also be filled with freight that is being carried to another country. This is loaded through huge doors in the side of the plane (*right*).

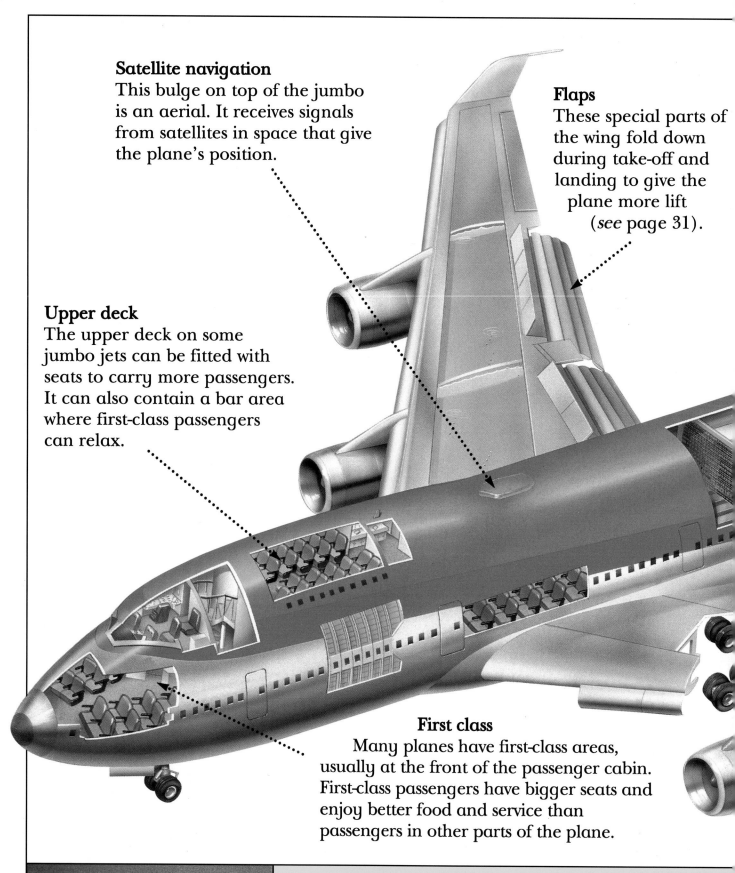

Satellite navigation
This bulge on top of the jumbo is an aerial. It receives signals from satellites in space that give the plane's position.

Flaps
These special parts of the wing fold down during take-off and landing to give the plane more lift (*see* page 31).

Upper deck
The upper deck on some jumbo jets can be fitted with seats to carry more passengers. It can also contain a bar area where first-class passengers can relax.

First class
Many planes have first-class areas, usually at the front of the passenger cabin. First-class passengers have bigger seats and enjoy better food and service than passengers in other parts of the plane.

JUMBO JET
The Boeing 747, or jumbo jet, is the largest passenger jet in the world. Some versions of the 747 can carry over 600 people!

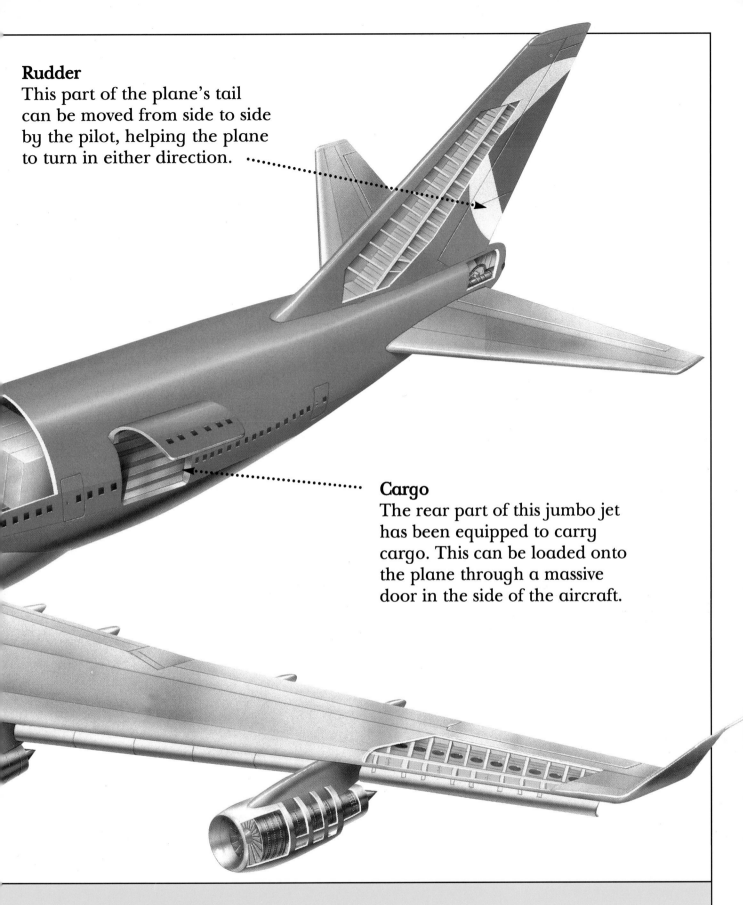

Rudder
This part of the plane's tail can be moved from side to side by the pilot, helping the plane to turn in either direction.

Cargo
The rear part of this jumbo jet has been equipped to carry cargo. This can be loaded onto the plane through a massive door in the side of the aircraft.

The bulge at the top of the plane contains the flight deck, where the pilots control the plane, and an extra passenger deck.

This version of a 747 combines a massive cargo hold and a passenger cabin so that it can carry both people and freight.

A lot of things occur

Airport

Airports can be massive places (*right*). Passengers board their planes at huge buildings called terminals. Once the plane is loaded and all of the passengers are on board, it is ready for takeoff.

Taxiing

The plane leaves the terminal and then moves, or taxis, to an available runway (*left*). The pilot then increases the power of the engines and the plane roars down the runway to take off and begin its flight.

during a jet's flight.

Air-traffic control

When the plane is in the air, air-traffic controllers on the ground (*left*) check its route and tell the pilots where to go. The plane's position is shown on a screen in front of them.

Landing

At the end of a flight, the plane descends and slows down its speed before coming down to land on a runway with its landing gear down (*below*).

What it takes to keep

The flight crew

Most jetliners are flown by two people, the pilot and the copilot. Some older planes have a third crew member, the flight engineer (*right*). The flight engineer checks that everything on the plane is working correctly.

Flight simulator

Pilots use special machines called flight simulators to learn how to fly and to practice even after they have qualified (*left*). Flight simulators mimic a flight in a plane — even its movements!

a jetliner in the air.

Engineers

To make sure that the plane is flying safely and smoothly, engineers check its parts between each flight (*above*).

Cabin steward

The cabin stewards look after the passengers during the flight. They make sure that the people are secured in their seats before takeoff and they serve them with food and drinks while the plane is in the air (*right*).

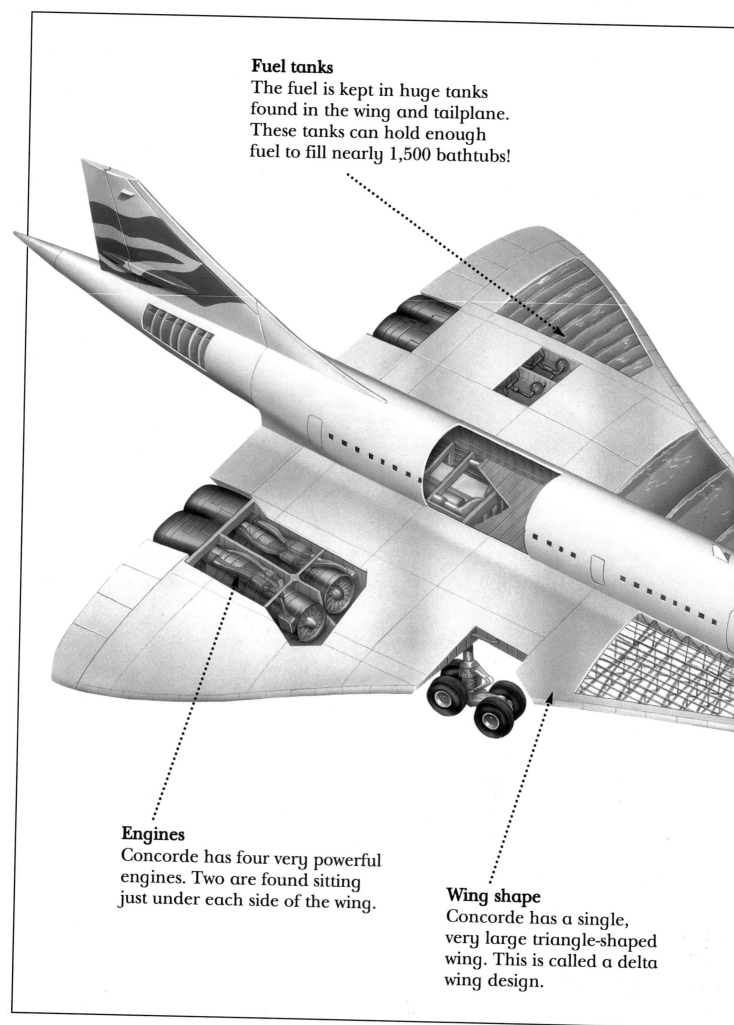

Fuel tanks
The fuel is kept in huge tanks
found in the wing and tailplane.
These tanks can hold enough
fuel to fill nearly 1,500 bathtubs!

Engines
Concorde has four very powerful
engines. Two are found sitting
just under each side of the wing.

Wing shape
Concorde has a single,
very large triangle-shaped
wing. This is called a delta
wing design.

Passenger cabin
The slim body of Concorde means that it can only carry 144 passengers.

CONCORDE

Concorde is the fastest jetliner in the world. It can fly at 1,360 mph (2,180 km/h) — that's twice as fast as the speed of sound. Because of this, Concorde can cross the Atlantic Ocean between Europe and the United States in just three hours! When it travels faster than the speed of sound, it creates a sonic boom. This bang has worried many people and has meant that Concorde is banned from flying faster than sound over land.

The Nose
Concorde's pointed nose is hinged so that it droops during landing and takeoff. This lets the pilots see the ground.

Preparing a jetliner

Refueling

An airliner uses a lot of fuel during each flight. Before it can take off for the next flight more fuel is pumped into its fuel tanks from gas tankers (*above*).

Luggage

Once the plane has come to a stop, the passengers' luggage is unloaded from the cargo hold (*right*). Once empty, the luggage for the next flight can be loaded on board.

for the next flight.

Safety checks

Before a jetliner can take off, all parts of it must be checked by engineers (*see* pages 16-17). These checks include looking at the plane's undercarriage to see if anything has been damaged or worn (*right*).

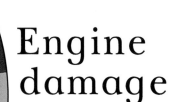

Engine damage

Air mechanics will also check the working parts inside a jet engine to see if they have become worn or damaged (*left*).

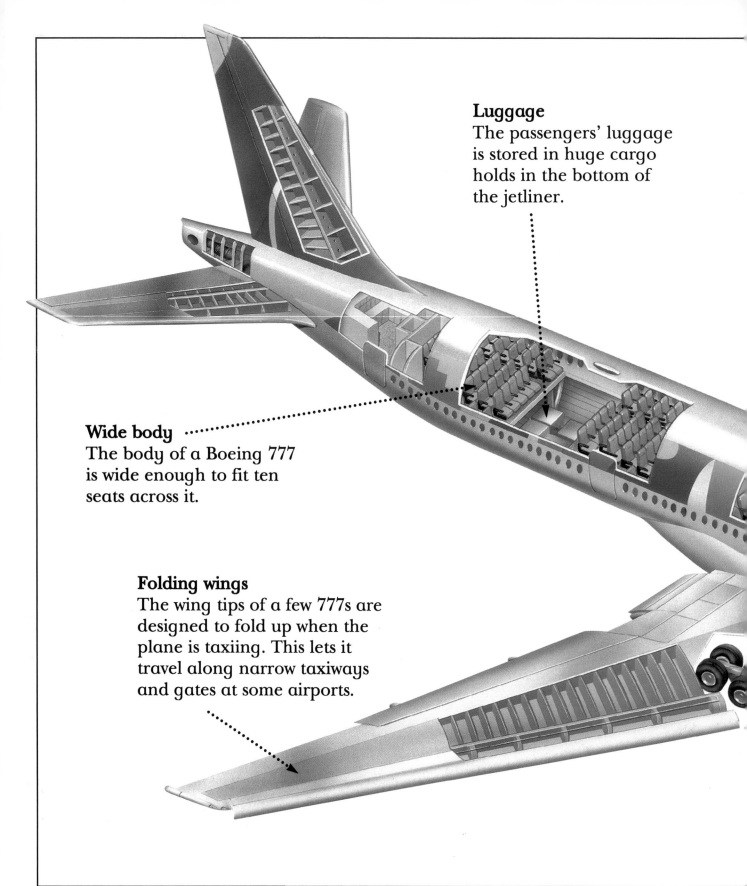

Luggage
The passengers' luggage is stored in huge cargo holds in the bottom of the jetliner.

Wide body
The body of a Boeing 777 is wide enough to fit ten seats across it.

Folding wings
The wing tips of a few 777s are designed to fold up when the plane is taxiing. This lets it travel along narrow taxiways and gates at some airports.

BOEING 777

The Boeing 777 is one of the most modern jetliners in use today. Using the latest technology and extremely powerful

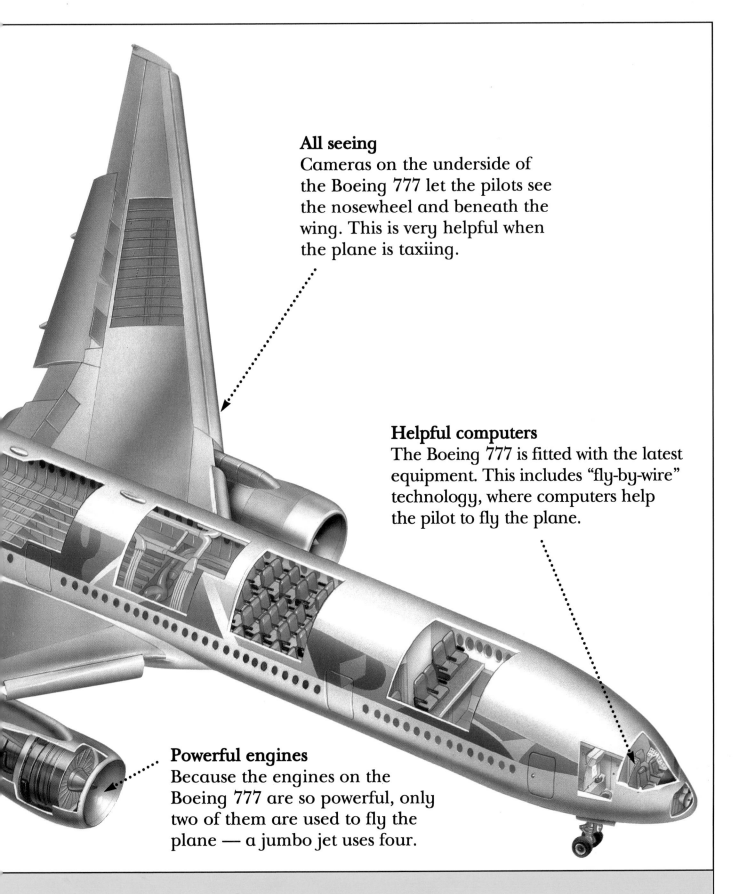

All seeing
Cameras on the underside of the Boeing 777 let the pilots see the nosewheel and beneath the wing. This is very helpful when the plane is taxiing.

Helpful computers
The Boeing 777 is fitted with the latest equipment. This includes "fly-by-wire" technology, where computers help the pilot to fly the plane.

Powerful engines
Because the engines on the Boeing 777 are so powerful, only two of them are used to fly the plane — a jumbo jet uses four.

engines, this new jetliner is far more efficient and a lot less expensive to run than the much older Boeing 747 (*see* pages 12-13). Inside its extra-wide body, the Boeing 777 can carry up to 550 passengers — nearly as many as a jumbo jet!

Many things make

Firefighters

Airport firefighters (*left*) have to wear special suits when they are tackling a blaze. These suits protect them from the heat of an aircraft fire.

Fire trucks

All airports have fire trucks (*below*) in case of an emergency. These trucks can race quickly to the scene and cover the fire with a thick blanket of foam.

flying very safe.

The black box

Inside every jetliner are some boxes that record the plane's actions. They are called black boxes (*right*). They are built to be tough so that, in the event of an accident, they can be recovered and investigators can find out what went wrong.

Escape slide

If an aircraft is in trouble on the ground, the passengers and crew may need to get out quickly. Special chutes inflate on the sides of the plane (*above*) and the people can slide down them to safety.

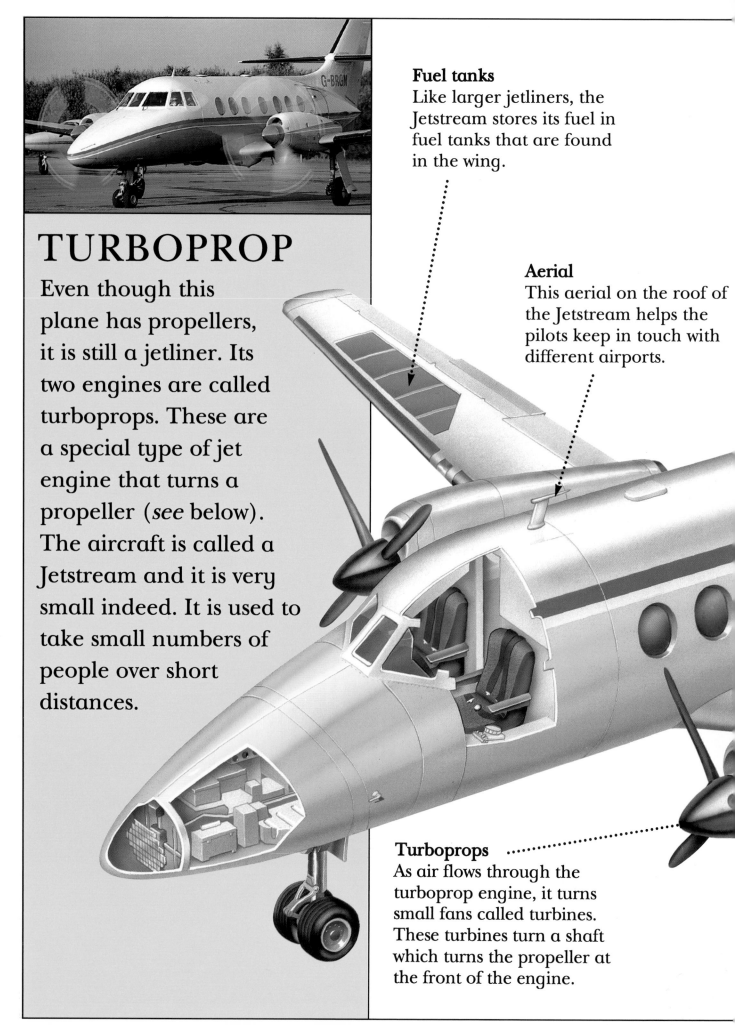

Fuel tanks
Like larger jetliners, the Jetstream stores its fuel in fuel tanks that are found in the wing.

Aerial
This aerial on the roof of the Jetstream helps the pilots keep in touch with different airports.

TURBOPROP

Even though this plane has propellers, it is still a jetliner. Its two engines are called turboprops. These are a special type of jet engine that turns a propeller (*see* below). The aircraft is called a Jetstream and it is very small indeed. It is used to take small numbers of people over short distances.

Turboprops
As air flows through the turboprop engine, it turns small fans called turbines. These turbines turn a shaft which turns the propeller at the front of the engine.

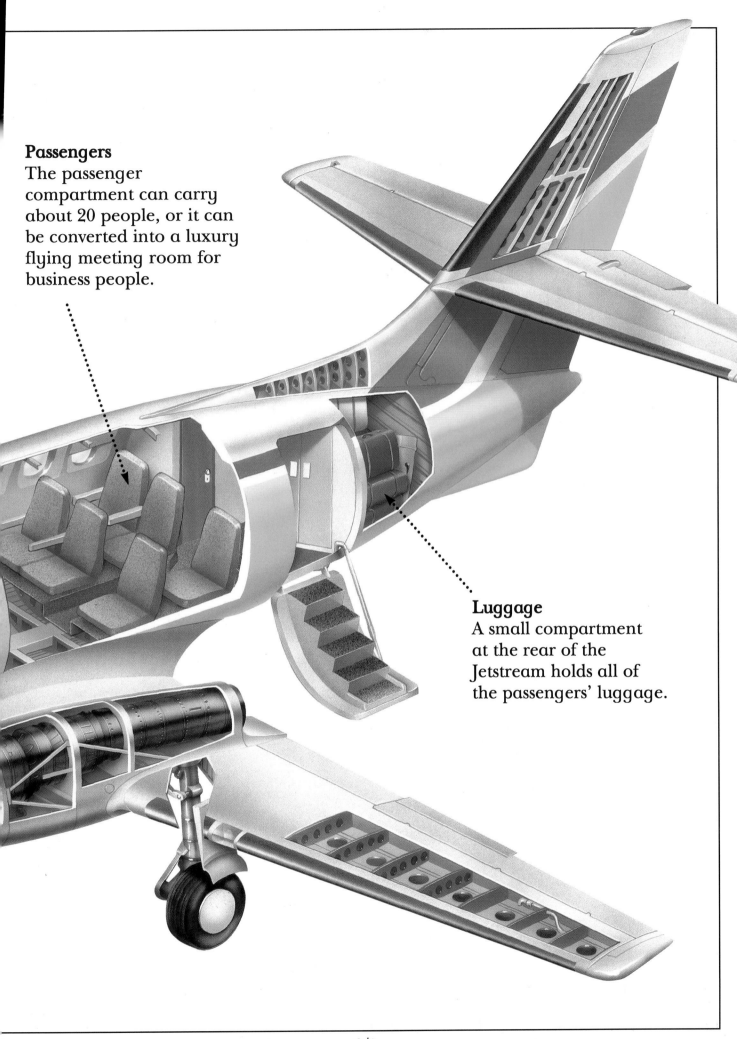

Passengers
The passenger compartment can carry about 20 people, or it can be converted into a luxury flying meeting room for business people.

Luggage
A small compartment at the rear of the Jetstream holds all of the passengers' luggage.

Jetliners are used for

Hide and seek

This plane (*below*) has been developed from an old jetliner. It is used by the British Royal Navy to search for enemy ships and submarines. It is also used in air-sea rescue, to find sailors and ships that are lost at sea.

Flight deck

Business jets

Very small jets, such as this one (*left*), can be used to carry business people from meeting to meeting.

a number of jobs.

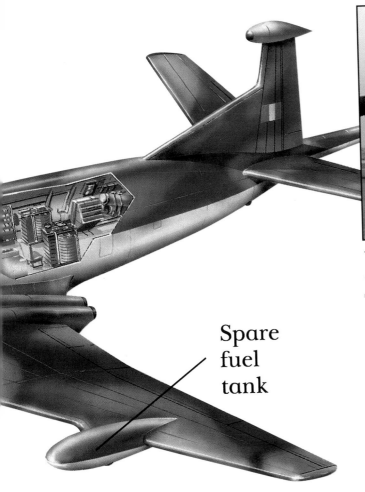

Spare fuel tank

Heavy lifting

This Galaxy transport jet (*above*) is used by the military. Its huge body contains an enormous cargo hold. The plane can carry troops, equipment, armored vehicles, and even tanks!

Air Force One

Any plane that the President of the United States flies in carries the call-sign "Air Force One." Typically, the President flies in a specially converted Boeing 747 (*right*).

UNITED STATES OF AMERICA

Fantastic Facts

• The world's first jetliner was the de Haviland Comet. It first carried passengers in May 1952 on a flight from England to Italy.

• The world's busiest airport is O'Hare airport in Chicago. In 1996, it handled 909,593 aircraft movements and an amazing 69,153,528 people passed through its gates.

• Edwards Air Force Base in the United States has the world's longest runway. It stretches for 7.5 miles (11.9 km) in the desert of California.

• In March 1989, a Russian Antonov An-225 lifted a cargo weighing a staggering 156 tons — that's the same as lifting over fifty elephants!

Jet words

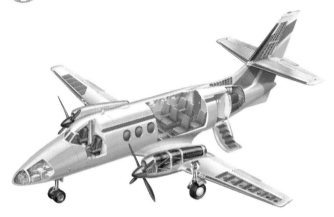

Ailerons

These are found on the rear of the wing. The pilot moves them up and down to make the plane bank and turn.

Flight deck

The part of a plane from where the pilot controls the jet.

Fly-by-wire

Some jets may be fitted with fly-by-wire technology. This means that a computer helps the pilot to fly the plane.

Jet engine

An engine that moves a plane forward by creating a jet of fast-moving gases.

Lift

The force created when air flows quickly over a specially shaped wing. This force pushes a plane up into the air.

Rudder

A part of the fin at the rear of the plane. The pilot can move this back and forth to help the plane turn.

Taxiing

The movement of a plane along the ground.

Turboprop

A special type of engine that uses a jet engine to turn a propeller.

Index

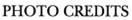

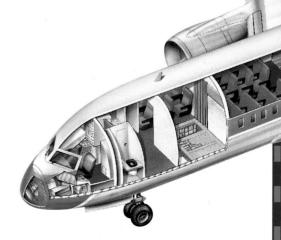